MY KARATE ADVENTURE

Leo Pecarina

Belle Pepper Illustrations

STUDIO OF BOOKS
THE SPACE FOR YOUR MESSAGE

Studio of Books LLC
5900 Balcones Drive Suite 100
Austin, Texas 78731
www.studioofbooks.org
Hotline: (254) 800-1183

Ordering Information:
Special discounts are available on quantity purchases by corporations, associations, and others. For details, contact the publisher at the address above.

Printed in the United States of America.

ISBN-13:   Softcover   978-1-968491-98-7
             eBook   978-1-968491-99-4

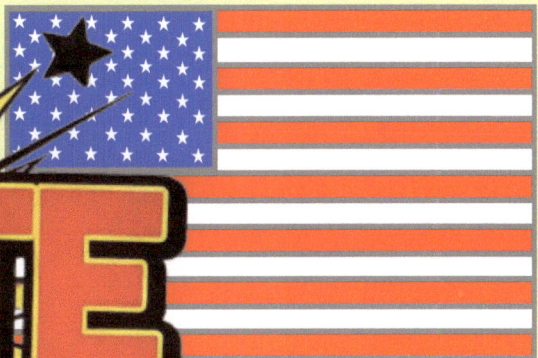

Hi, my name is Leo. I love going on adventures and learning new things. This is a book about my adventure to learn karate.

When I was 6 years old, I went to Minnesota in the summer to visit my family. It was a long drive across the country but I got to see some really cool things.

We drove by my favorite place in Tennessee, Raccoon Mountain! One time I went camping there for the 4th of July and I made new friends. We caught fireflies and put them in a jar.

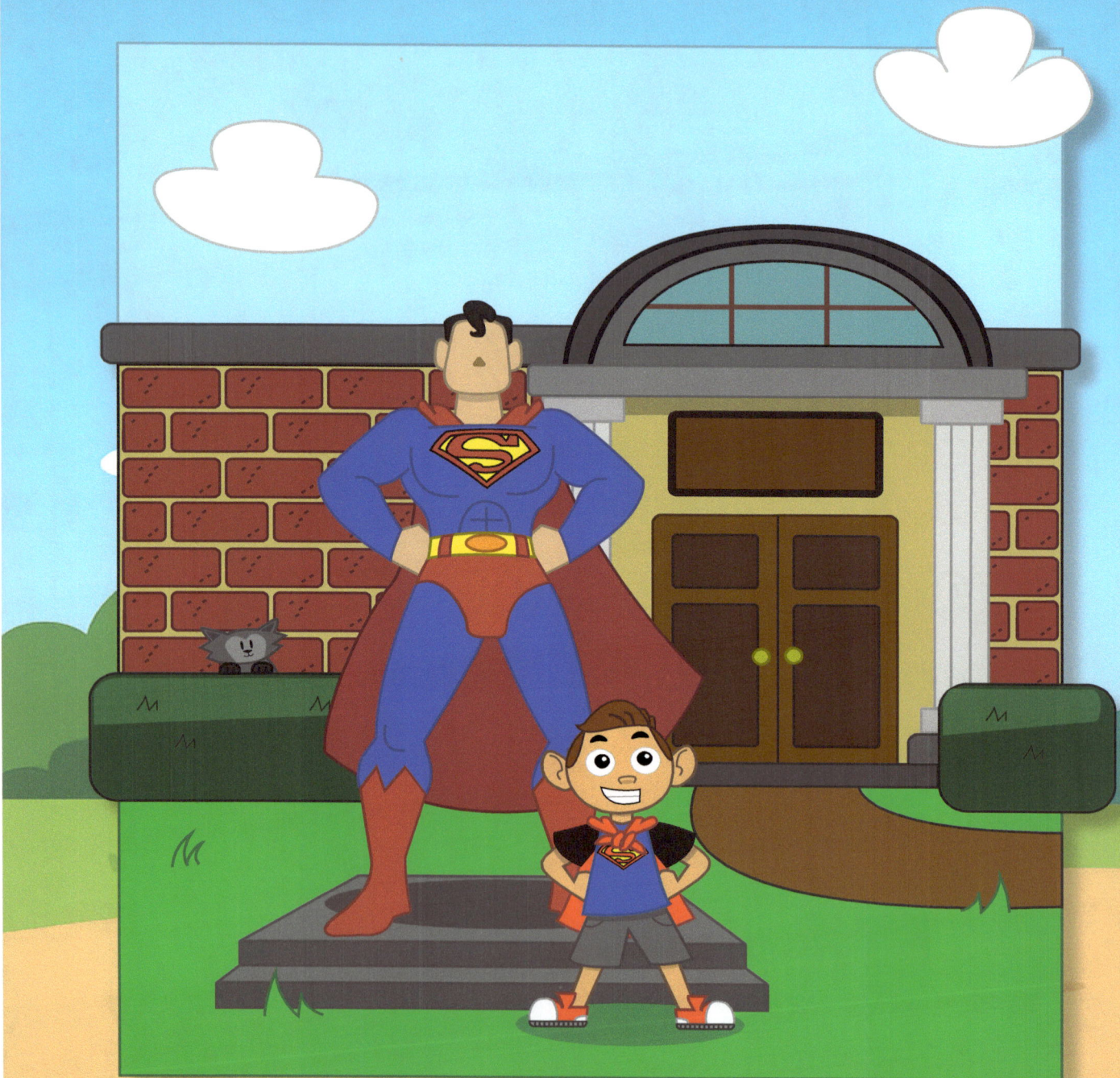

We stopped in Metropolis, Illinois to visit the world's largest Superman! It was so cool to see the comic book shops and the Superman museum. Sometimes I pretend that I'm Superman.

When I went through Iowa, I learned how to make ice cream from my friends. They had a freezer so big you could walk inside, but it was really cold! I love walking in giant freezers.

When I got to Minnesota my cousins were so happy to see me they almost knocked me to the ground trying to give me hugs. I was really happy to see them too!

They asked me to start taking karate classes but I wasn't sure if I should do it because I didn't know if I would like it. After a few classes, I got to break a board with my hand and get my very first white belt! I knew I would love it.

I went to karate class everyday because I wanted to be a black belt someday. It was really hard work but it was a lot of fun too.

My cousins already had their black belt so they could help teach my classes. I think karate is fun for everyone because I saw old people and kids doing karate at the same time.

After working really hard all summer, I graduated from my white belt to my gold belt. I was really happy and my family was really proud of me for working so hard.

The next summer, we went back to Minnesota so I could keep taking karate classes. This year was even more challenging because I had to learn new forms.

These classes were different because I wasn't just learning about karate, I was learning about respect, discipline, and responsibility. My karate teacher told me that if I want to graduate to higher belts, I would need to be listening to my parents and helping out at home, doing my chores, and being respectful.

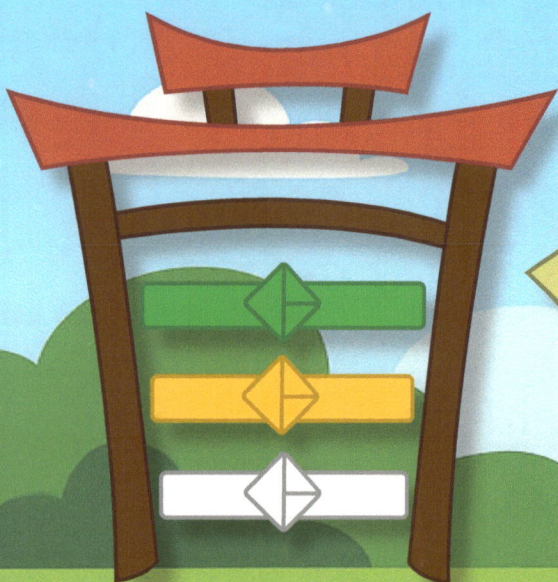

Goals

- [ ] clean my room
- [ ] earn a black stripe
- [ ] show respect at school

When I graduated from my gold belt to my green belt, it was a little harder to remember all of my forms and one-step moves. When I was learning my green belt I had to learn more discipline. I even had a goal sheet and learned how to set goals.

Goals

- ✓ clean my room
- ✓ earn a black stripe
- ✓ show respect at school

I learned that it takes a lot of strength and a lot of practice to get higher belts in karate. It was really hard to be disciplined every single day but I was really happy when I completed my goals. My family was really proud of me.

I graduated to my purple belt and that was really fun. I got to break more boards with my own hands and I learned new karate moves. The most important thing that I learned about karate is "Might For Right". That means we don't use karate to fight people, we just use it to protect ourselves from danger.

I am learning so much from karate. It teaches me to be responsible for myself and my actions, like being polite and being kind to people, and listening to my parents. It teaches me to have discipline to do the things I know I need to do, like putting away my clothes and brushing my teeth and helping with my chores without being told. Most of all, it's a lot of fun and really good exercise.

I love going on my adventures and learning new things to share them with you. I'm working really hard to get my black belt someday, maybe you will too!

www.ingramcontent.com/pod-product-compliance
Lightning Source LLC
Chambersburg PA
CBHW061143030426
42335CB00002B/86